Table of Contents

I0415382

Printed in the United States of America

First printing, 2019

ISBN 9781096718963

PreCombatCheck.com

Everything in this book is publicly accessible. There is no secret information. Operational security has been taken *very* seriously.

This book is dedicated to those who choose to fight for

their country.

Mission Statement

The purpose of this book is to teach you about life, strength, and joining the military. The information covered is to help you understand, from beginning to end, the process of being a service member. The goal is to set you up for success. After reading this, you should have realistic expectations of what you are getting into. Use this guide to make the best decision for you *and* your family.

When I joined the military, I had no idea what I was doing. All I knew was that I wanted to fight in a war and jump out of airplanes. It would have helped me a lot if someone had told me the things I cover in this book. I hope you find the information useful and easy to understand. Apply this knowledge to succeed in the military and life as a whole.

In the military, I was assigned to the 75th Ranger Regiment. I went on five combat deployments. Following my service time, I worked as a security contractor. During that period, I crossed paths with many veterans. This is my way of sharing with you everything I have learned in a nutshell.

There is a lot of information available about the military. However, things can be confusing when you do not know who to listen to. Most civilians do not know the differences between the Marines and the Army. Special operations is also a topic that is not really understood. Do you know what the distinctions are between Rangers and Special Forces? Do you know what benefits you are entitled to after you get out? Keep reading, you will learn how everything is broken down.

Recruiters are a great source to learn from about joining. However, the truth is a person does not enter the military to become a recruiter. Frankly, a lot of them are not there by choice. Which means, they will only tell you what you want to hear. I am a veteran who is not affiliated with any group. This means I will share the good *and* bad sides of signing up. This book is intended to be a simple, honest guide that covers all the basics as if I am talking to you in person.

What you will learn:

- What a warrior is

- Where strength comes from

- Being proactive. Choose to live by choice

- Only worrying about what you can control

- Tips to succeed. Common mistakes to learn from

- Mental health. PTSD, depression, and suicide

- Understanding the structure of the military,

  including the special operation units

- The enlistment process

- Getting out. Transitioning back to the civilian world

- Several basic workout structures

Introduction

In the summer of 2008, I decided to join the military. I had zero knowledge of what I was getting into. Initially, my goal was to become a marine. I thought they were the fiercest warriors, at least that is what their commercials told me. That dream was short lived. My only visit to a marine recruiter did not go well. The recruiter did not even bother to lift his head up when I walked into his office. As I started to close the door, another recruiter ran out to catch me. He quickly sat me down.

The recruiter began to tell me about their uniforms. He then explained how hard basic training was. I was very discouraged because my sole reason to join was to go fight in a war. The information he shared was irrelevant to accomplishing my goals. Deflated from what I learned, I started to walk out of the recruitment center.

Next door was the Army recruiter's office. A sergeant pulled me in and shared a story from his time in Iraq. His convoy was ambushed on a mission, and he responded by calling in an airstrike. That was all I needed to hear, I was sold. After listening to my goals, he pointed me towards the direction of trying to become a Ranger. Even though I had no idea what a Ranger was, I signed up. It turned out to be a tremendous life-changing decision that has shaped me into the man I am today. I appreciated the honesty of that recruiter and the story he told me. I would like to start by sharing a story with you.

A war story

The helicopters roared as we flew away from our base. As always, I said goodbye to my family. Losing all hope was freedom. That acceptance would let me fight until my death if I had to. Under the cover of darkness, we raced towards our objective. I closed my eyes for a moment, trying to sneak in some rest before the night began.

Startled by the three-minute call, I got ready to fight. Our bird touched down with the usual bounce. The ramp lowered, and we sprinted off. We had to be quick because the target compound was a short distance away. I trailed behind a squad leader and one of his team leaders. As we got close, I saw movement inside the building. The guys ahead of me headed down an alleyway.

A man from inside the compound hurriedly ran down a flight of stairs from a second story room. He came out through the front gate. In his language, I yelled, "Hands up, or I will shoot!". Startled by my presence, he hesitated. He began to lift his hands but quickly dropped them, figuring running was a better option. The man was not armed. I grabbed the attention of my platoon mates, and we followed pursuit.

A plane from above had spotted another guy running away. I saw a light from overhead highlight his position. We caught up to the first guy, who I initially saw come out of the compound. We took him under custody. The second runner was about a kilometer away. He took a fighting position at the base of a mountain. A few of us ran to chase him down.

The radio came alive with a report. Another helicopter was headed to pick up the second runner. As I ran up a hill, I heard rotors chopping through the air. The bird flew right over me, its shadow from the moonlight was cast along the village. The three of us that chased the second runner set up support by fire. We watched as the bird approached its mark.

The helicopter hovered at the base of a mountain. A rope was tossed out of the bird. A squad of Rangers began to slide down for a quick entry. The targeted individual was hiding behind a large rock. He was armed and ready to fight. The first guy to get down on the ground was a fire team leader.

The enemy combatant decided to peak his head out. He was most likely trying to see where the people chasing him were. There was a moment of silence. All I saw was one quick flash. Threat neutralized. The fight was over in an instant. Upon completing our objective, we loaded up on helicopters and headed back to our base. Once we arrived there, we prepared for the next mission.

Why join?

I did not get a shot off on that objective from the story I just shared. However, the experience was intense and exciting. Nights like that are why I joined the military. Each person will have their own reasons for signing up. Join because *you* choose to. Know *why* you want to be there.

It is easy to want the glory. Many people only think about the positives when signing up. There are downsides to being in the military as well. You willingly give up individual freedoms to be there. Several examples are, your future is based on the needs of the military. Also, you will have to adhere to the strict rules and standards of the government.

Every single job has its downsides. Whether you work as a computer programmer, become a doctor, or are a dog handler in Special Forces. The question you need to ask yourself is, do the positives outweigh the negatives? All the difficult times become worth it when you do something like riding in a helicopter. During the flight, the bird may bank hard in one direction. You will be facing the ground, wondering how you did not fall out. Another example is if you hear a fighter jet swoop in and drop a giant bomb. Those are the experiences you can not get anywhere else.

Being in the military is challenging. If you decide to join, it will be difficult. The result will lead to seeing who you really are. You will gain strength and confidence in yourself. Completing tasks and missions will become a part of your nature. You will be able to lead people and take control when you need to. Stressful situations will be much more tolerable. You will learn universal principles and live out excellent core values. The work you do will have a global impact. You will belong to a tribe and be a part of something much bigger than yourself. The whole process will make you more capable as an individual. If you ask me, I say the juice is worth the squeeze. However, you have to decide for yourself.

The Call of the Warrior

Warriors sprint to a firefight expecting death. Are you one of those people? This question may cause some uncertainty and doubt. If you have not been tested, you know that there is a chance you may fail. Every single person that signs up has to accept this fear. Those bold enough will put themselves out there to see if they have what it takes.

This great country needs people to stand up and fight. Sacrifice is necessary to protect the American way of life. Freedom and democracy come with a price. Do you hear the call to become a warrior? If you do, listen to it and go fight. Neglect it, and you will always wonder if you could have made it. You only have one life, see who you really are.

Common reasons people join the military:

- Simply to fight (if this is you, go try out for a special operations unit)

- Country

- To take care of family

- Faith

- Benefits such as school, pay, and health coverage

- To become a naturalized citizen

Several things to think about before joining:

- Death or severe injuries are possible
- If you sign up solely to fight, realize there is a chance you may never see combat
- Most days will not be fun or glamorous
- Sleep is the last priority. Food may be limited and terrible
- You are not on your time
- It is a difficult place to be. You will be tested physically, mentally, spiritually, socially, and emotionally
- Events and situations can be traumatic
- You will be away from home a lot
- It is very stressful for families, especially if you have kids
- If you make a mistake, you could be kicked out of the military

"Fate whispers to the warrior, 'You cannot withstand the storm.' The warrior whispers back, 'I am the storm.'"

-Unknown

Chapter 1 - Becoming a Warrior

A man possessed

Imagine a massive attack on a company of army soldiers. The enemy strikes with six tanks, along with hundreds of men. The company commander tells his troops to withdraw back to the woods. He picks up his radio and starts calling in artillery. A friendly tank nearby gets hit and is set on fire. The crew hops out. They withdraw back to the woods from fear that the tank might blow up.

The leader orders for more artillery to be dropped. He sees a machine gun on top of the burning tank. Even though bullets are coming in from three sides, he jumps on

19

the abandoned vehicle and starts engaging. Unleashing fury, he kills dozens of combatants. This return of fire stuns the attackers, causing the siege to slow down. Enemy tanks are forced to pull back because they lose ground support.

An hour passes, and this man is still fighting off the attack by himself. The enemy uses every gun they have. They even come as close as ten yards to him. It does not matter what they throw, he stands his ground. A bullet penetrates his leg. Wounded, he keeps fighting.

Finally, he runs out of ammunition and retreats back to the woods. There he comes up with a plan while refusing medical care. The counterattack is successful and causes the enemy to withdraw. The company leader ends up killing many enemy combatants and saving friendly lives. His actions deny the enemies objective of taking the woods by trying to encircle their position. [1]

That is a remarkable story, right? The guy sounds like he is six feet eight inches tall, rocking a giant beard, and holding two axes. The truth is, this man only stood at five feet five inches. He weighed a mere one hundred and twelve pounds. When this event took place, he was only nineteen. Initially, he had trouble enlisting due to his physical size.

This story might sound an awful lot like a comic book superhero. However, the events described above actually happened. The real *Captain America* was named Audie Murphy. He is one of the most decorated soldiers in American history, receiving *every* medal available.

Audie Murphy was not the ideal size for a soldier. He was not the biggest, fastest, or strongest guy. However, what this man possessed was much more important, the

Warrior Spirit. This is how he stood in the face of danger and fought back regardless of his appearance.

"When asked after the war why he had seized the machine gun and had taken on an entire company of German infantry, he replied, 'They were killing my friends.'" [2]

Audie Murphy's reason for fighting was simply for love for his brothers. He risked his life because his tribe meant more than himself. His foundation was set on a stable belief system. What are you willing to fight for? Is that belief so strong that you would die for it? If you answered yes, then seek this spirit. You too can become fearless.

The Warrior Spirit

The Warrior Spirit is founded in the very essence of nature. It all comes down to survival of the fittest. A warrior is an individual who is willing to risk everything for their tribe to live on. They are responsible for the protection of their community. This duty is not for the faint of heart.

Only in the face of grave danger will you see what someone is made of. There will be people who you can trust with your life. Unfortunately, there are others you will not want to be around when things get rough. It is only during difficult trials that this spirit is revealed.

Anyone can possess the Warrior Spirit. It is a deep embodiment of courage, strength, and purpose. There must be an understanding of yourself and knowing where you belong. You have to establish a solid belief system and be strong mentally, physically, and spiritually. It takes true self-mastery. You do not need to be in Delta Force to be a warrior. With that said, this spirit is commonly found throughout the special operations community.

Chasing the white elephant

During the Civil War, soldiers would go on patrols expecting to fight. They all wondered how they would react when shots were fired. For some soldiers, a lot of time would pass before they ever saw combat. Some people started to think that war was not real. The desire to fight became a fantasy because it seemed to be an elusive mythical beast. It became known as "chasing the white elephant."

My main reason for enlisting was to prove to myself that I was a warrior. The goal was to find the mythical "white elephant." I prayed for a firefight, so I could see what I was truly made of. Was I courageous or a coward? Was I strong or weak? I wanted to know, and not just think, that I possessed the Warrior Spirit. Joining the military during wartime was the best way to find out.

Living by a creed

Creeds are the foundation of a group. Each military branch and their respective special operation units have their own creed. It is a written mission statement that incorporates the goals, principles, and values that summarize what an individual must possess to be a part of that tribe. At Ranger School, you say the Ranger Creed every day. Repeating it will ingrain those words into the back of your skull. The purpose is to become what you say. Next is an example of a military creed.

The Ranger Creed

Recognizing that I volunteered as a Ranger, fully knowing the hazards of my chosen profession, I will always endeavor to uphold the prestige, honor, and high esprit de corps of the Rangers.

Acknowledging the fact that a Ranger is a more elite Soldier who arrives at the cutting edge of battle by land, sea, or air, I accept the fact that as a Ranger my country expects me to move further, faster and fight harder than any other Soldier.

Never shall I fail my comrades. I will always keep myself mentally alert, physically strong and morally straight and I will shoulder more than my share of the task whatever it may, one-hundred-percent and then some.

Gallantly will I show the world that I am a specially selected and well-trained Soldier. My courtesy to superior officers, neatness of dress and care of equipment shall set the example for others to follow.

Energetically will I meet the enemies of my country. I shall defeat them on the field of battle for I am better trained and will fight with all my might. Surrender is not a Ranger word. I will never leave a fallen comrade to fall into the hands of the enemy and under no circumstances will I ever embarrass my country.

Readily will I display the intestinal fortitude required to fight on to the Ranger objective and complete the mission though I be the lone survivor.

Rangers lead the way! [3]

Your own creed

A truly strong person lives by their own creed. This personal mission statement is comprised of the group you belong to (tribe), your intent (goals), principles you live by (rules of life), and core values (priorities). If you are not sure who you are, start by writing your own creed.

Be centered on your creed. Set it as your foundation. Fall back on what you believe when things get hard. If you do, no storm that passes will be able to knock you over. You will be the same inside and out. The creed is who you are, where you come from, and where you are going. Live by your own creed.

Creed outline (refine it over time as you grow)

I am _____. (Your name)

I come from _____. (Your roots. Where your family came from)

I belong _____. (This is your tribe. Examples can be family, friends, or platoon)

I believe in _____. (Your paradigm. How you believe the world works)

I live by these principles _____. (Universal rules of life. For example, the only thing you can control is how you react, or how everything is temporary)

My core values are _____. (How you prioritize what is important. Examples are integrity, respect, duty, and selflessness)

I am going to be_____. (Write down your goals. Examples are to be successful, educated, strong, a teacher, scientist, SEAL, sniper)

Chapter 2 - Strength

Strength can be broken down into three categories. The main areas are mental, physical, and spiritual. It is essential to be well rounded. A person who is not physically strong will have serious trouble carrying their weight. Someone spiritually weak may lose purpose quickly. Lastly, an individual who lacks mental toughness will give up when things get too hard.

Where does strength come from?

Strength comes from the proactive pursuit of self-mastery. This should be the goal of every single individual, regardless if you are in the military or not. To become a master of yourself, you must understand and know your limits. You also have to sharpen yourself mentally, physically, and spiritually. This requires daily work. It is a grind that has to be balanced.

The refining process takes time. Every day you need to work on yourself. Eventually, you will become an immovable force. You will be able to accomplish anything you set your mind to. I am not saying you will inherit superpowers (go to Ranger School for that). You will know what you are made of. You will be aware of what you are good at and have an understanding of your limits. This will allow you to become the best human you can possibly be.

You can become unshakable. With that said, failure is inevitable. As the old saying goes, "It is not how many times you get knocked down, but how many times you get up." Learning from mistakes will help you avoid the same problem in the future. Grow from failures.

Reach your full potential. It takes hard work, dedication, and consistency. Start by starving the ego and feeding the soul. Decide that no matter what, you will be honest inside and out. That virtue is called integrity. It gives you a place to start.

After you show personal integrity, you must respect and love yourself for who you are. Confidence comes from inside. The words you tell yourself are what you will start believing. Negative thoughts are destructive. This type of thinking can also lead to depression. Think positive.

Accept yourself as you are. You can not control where you came from, how you look, or what your natural talents are. All of these traits are genetic. They are based on your family tree and environment. Just let go. Smile at yourself when you look in the mirror. Think of who you want to become. Make that vision your primary goal.

The next step is in understanding how to contribute to each aspect of strength. Work on it daily. Over time, you will become that which you set out to be. You can not change the past, but the future can be better. The choice is yours. The only time to start is now.

"I will always keep myself mentally alert, physically strong and morally straight" - The Ranger Creed

Mentally

Expectations are everything. If you have the right mindset, based on universal principles, there will be no surprises. Being rational will give you the ability to adapt. An example of a universal principle is that the past is a part of you, but it is not who you are. There are rules to how the universe works.

Mental fortitude can help you surpass your physical limitations. Charlie Beckwith is the founder of the military unit called "Delta Force." In his memoirs, he explains the selection process for new recruits. The final exercise is a forty-mile hike. At the twelve to fourteen-hour mark, the body is so exhausted that it ends up failing. This last long journey is solely a test of mental strength.

Conquer the situation in your head. Everything else will follow. Every trial you go through will be eighty-percent mental. If you can master yourself, then no task will be too hard. There will be no mountain too big to climb. Any mission can be accomplished.

Physically

Working out is a part of the daily military routine. It is equally important to maintain a good diet and to get proper sleep. You have to balance all three to be healthy and become physically strong. Lacking in one area will affect how you perform.

Consistency is key. It is the most important characteristic to possess to get in good shape. Work out regularly, and you will see results. The next most important attribute is intensity. The harder you work out, the more you will benefit. Follow these two fundamental principles, and you will become fit.

Every military member will have to take a physical fitness test (PFT). Each branch has its own standards. The base exercises are all the same. The core workouts are push-ups, sit-ups, running, and pull-ups (this exercise is tested only by a few branches and units). On top of the basic PFT, each branch has some sort of fitness event. The activities in the extended PFT are the deadlift, bench press, three hundred meter sprint, rope climb, long jump, and many others. The extensive fitness tests vary from each branch and unit.

The point being is that you need to get into shape. The more fit you are, the better you will perform on missions and the less stress a PFT will be. Additionally, you will have more opportunities presented to you. For example, people with the top PFT scores may be offered different military schools, like Airborne or sniper school. Maxing out on your PFT will also give you promotion points. Those points can help you rank up faster. The higher the rank, the more responsibility and pay you will receive. There are only positive things that come from being in great shape.

Different ways to work out

- Running
- Rucking
- Swimming
- Biking
- Body weight exercises
- Lifting weights
- Sports

Running - It is the single most important exercise you should master. If you can run, you can succeed. Humans are the best long distance runners out of any animal... on the planet! Today, with modern vehicles, there is much less need to run. In the military, it is essential.

Cardiovascular exercise is at the core of every physical activity you will do. Anyone can become a good runner if they practice consistently. Keep in mind that the more specialized the unit you try out for, the faster you will need to run. Time standards may be stressful. Use that pressure to push yourself.

If you have not gone running in a long time, try by starting slow and easy. Do not think you have to run a marathon your very first run. Pick a short route and try to run the whole time. Each session you go running, attempt to run a little further. The more you do it, the better you will be at it. You do not need fancy shoes or expensive clothes to start (or honestly ever). Put on the clothes you already have and just go for it. If you are breathing too hard, then slow down. Set a pace where you can think while you run. You are only racing yourself.

Push-ups - Get in the prone position. Lower, then raise your body. Accomplish this by using your arms and midsection as a whole. The goal is to have your elbows bend to the point where you break the ninety-degree angle. Practice by touching your chest to the ground and pushing yourself back up to where your elbows are fully extended.

Sit-ups - Sit on your butt and lay your back on the ground. Lift your torso to an upright position without lifting your arms or feet. A key to doing a lot of sit-ups is by having a reliable partner who holds your ankles down tight. Waste as little energy as you can on your way down. Throw your body back, and let gravity do its job. As soon as your shoulder blades touch the ground, bounce back up. Use that momentum to carry you into your next repetition.

Pull-ups - Grab a bar with both hands. Let your body hang free. Use your arms and back to pull your body up. The goal is to reach the point where your chin goes above the bar. When you train, try and touch your chest to the bar. Practice and do a lot of repetitions to be good at it.

Rucking - The purpose of rucking is to simulate conducting a ground patrol for a mission. Military members need to be able to cover a large area on foot. Every individual has to carry their own gear, food, and water.

Practice by walking with a backpack on. Add items like water bottles in your pack to increase the difficulty. Running with heavy weight in your bag can cause stress fractures, so be cautious. Practice by walking briskly. When the time comes to do it for a test, or on a mission, do what is needed to succeed. Pack the heavy weight on top, so your upper back and shoulders take the load. If not, your lower back will hurt. Tighten the pack as high as it can go. Use the hip and chest straps when you can. They help to distribute the weight.

Shooting - Every person entering the military will learn how to shoot. All members are there to fight and need to know how to operate their weapon systems. If you have never touched a firearm before joining, you will be fine. The first time I shot a gun was in basic training with a drill sergeant screaming in my ear.

All weapons can be lethal when handled irresponsibly. Improper use can cause severe injury or death. Always treat a gun like it is loaded. A firearm will not randomly go off by itself. It is due to human error that these negligent discharges happen. Be responsible and take safety *very* seriously.

Fundamentals of marksmanship:

1. Steady position
2. Aim
3. Breathe control
4. Trigger squeeze

Practice and master these four fundamentals. In most units, you may be very limited on range time. The special operation units offer a lot more courses, training, and time to practice.

Food

Food is fuel for the body. Eating healthy is very important. What you consume will affect your performance.

While you are in the military, you will be provided with a good selection of food. Take advantage of this and eat well.

Consistency is key. You have to eat well on the average to see the benefits. There are many diets out there. Many programs claim to be the ultimate way to intake food. At the end of the day, you need a certain amount of nutrients to stay alive and perform. You can make a very detailed food plan, meticulous down to the very gram. This may be essential for a bodybuilder. For the average military person, it is not necessary to be that extreme.

Eat a balanced diet. Make sure to consume a lot of protein and fats. Ideally, stay away from sugary foods such as candy, pies, brownies, and so on. Eating snacks once in a while is ok, just try not to overdo it. Listen to your body. Keep everything in moderation.

Food breakdown

Protein - It is the building block of growth. If you want to be healthy, make sure you eat something filled with protein every day. There is a simple rule to let you know how much protein to consume. Eat just over half of a gram of protein per body weight. For example, if you want to maintain a weight of one hundred pounds, eat sixty to eighty grams of protein per day. Any protein not used will be turned to fat and used as energy. [1]

- Good protein sources: Steak, chicken, fish, black beans, eggs, nuts, and quinoa
- Bad protein source: Processed Meats

Fats - A great source of energy. Fats are necessary to live. They provide vitamins and help keep your skin healthy.

Your body uses fat as energy after it burns through carbs. [2]

- <u>Good fat sources:</u> Cheese, avocados, walnuts, almonds, and olives
- <u>Bad fat sources:</u> Doughnuts, cakes, or anything deep fried

<u>Carbohydrates (Carbs)</u> - A source of energy from starches and sugars. Carbs are not a necessary part of the daily diet. Limit your carb intake to stay healthy. [3]

- <u>Good carb sources:</u> Brussel sprouts, broccoli, spinach, fruits
- <u>Bad carb sources:</u> Sugary cereals, bread, candy, and cookies

Water

Hydration - Water is the oil for the body. Drinking water is vital. Dehydration can cause many adverse effects on your health. Several consequences include fatigue, weak immune system, and even heart issues. There are many daily recommendations for staying hydrated. Each individual is different. If you are thirsty, drink water. If you have an event coming up, drink a lot of water. It is that simple. [4]

Sleep

Sleep is a commodity. In the military, you may be forced to stay up for extended periods. You will be asked to function as if you had enough sleep, it is no easy task. Sleeping nine hours a night is unrealistic to expect. Learning a little about the human sleep cycle can help. Even when limited on time, you may be able to get rest and help your body recover.

Current research has pointed towards catching up on sleep during the weekend as a myth. Just like physical fitness and diet, you need to be consistent to see good results. Ultimately, it is what you average overall. Two days may not be enough to make up for the lost time. [5]

Rapid eye movement (REM) - Sleep is when your body shuts down certain areas to recover. During this state of unconsciousness, your body rebuilds cells. It does this by releasing testosterone and human growth hormone. A human's natural sleep cycle occurs during the night. This goes along with something called the circadian rhythm.

The circadian rhythm is the natural cycle that everything in nature revolves around. [6]

The REM cycle has four phases. The average time to complete one cycle is ninety minutes. Try to sleep in one and a half hour increments. This is the optimal time for your body to complete a cycle. If you wake up without completing a cycle, you may feel tired and off. Your body may not have enough time to recover properly. Going back to bed only resets the cycle. [7]

It is difficult to make up for lost sleep. The more you break the cycle, the more you will compound the issues. Some side effects of prolonged lack of sleep are constant tiredness, dizziness, fatigue, weaker immune system, poor concentration, anxiety, irritability, memory loss, and more. Do your best to get proper rest.

<u>REM cycle stages (lasts around ninety minutes):</u>

- Rem 1: Laying down

- Rem 2: Light sleep

- Rem 3: Dream state

- Rem 4: Deep sleep

<u>Good habits to help you maximize on sleep:</u>

- Do not look at electronic screens one hour before sleeping

- Sleep in a pitch black room

- Sleep and wake up at the same time every day

- Listen to white noise if you are in a loud area (leave a fan on or play nature sounds)

- Use a blanket where you do not sweat, but stay warm

- Keep the room temperature cool

Spiritually

Recognize your place in the world. This will help you define your worldview and belief system. Purpose comes from knowing why you are doing something. If you know the *why* then the *how* will follow. Whether you follow a religion or not, you can still be spiritual. Being spiritual is trying to align yourself with nature. Religions are simply a manifestation of this concept.

Everyone is on their own personal journey. Know what you believe because *you* chose it. For example, understand *why* you want to join the military. What are you personally fighting for? When you take ownership, you will be confident in the route you choose. Take control by challenging your own belief system. Do your best to align it to reality.

Members of the Armed Forces have an assumed belief in the United States of America. The Constitution is what the nation collectively believes in. The military protects this way of living. Learn about what you believe and why. From there you will always know which side you are fighting for.

Chapter 3 - Tips for Success

There is a lot more going on than just shooting a gun. This chapter is to help you think about some of the small things. Aim to be well-rounded. Apply what you learn from these points to better yourself.

Be proactive

The power to choose what you do in life is yours. Be proactive and live deliberately. Know where you want to go to before you start. Starting with the end first will help you choose the best path. If you let someone else choose your route, you may be extremely dissatisfied when the results are not what you wanted.

Be authentic

Truly become what you are striving to be. Do not just imitate but become the real thing. With modern technology, people want results immediately. However, becoming an infantryman, pilot, or Navy SEAL takes a lot of time. It is hard work and a daily grind. You have to earn it. Do not cheat your way just so you can say you did it. If you cut corners, someone will recognize your lie and call you out. It takes dedication, commitment, and persistence. The result will be much more fulfilling.

Life guidelines:

- Live centered on universal principles

- Belong to a tribe

- Hold to your values

- Focus solely on goals and relationships

Root causes for stress and conflicts

<u>False expectations</u> - Disappointment is a result of things not going the way you thought it would. Align your expectations with reality.

<u>Miscommunication</u> - Another person can not know what you are thinking unless you outwardly express what you want. Do not assume anything. Communication is key.

Philosophy to live by

Be stoic. Be indifferent to things you can not control. Imagine you are trying to stop ocean waves from crashing onto the shore of a beach. No matter how hard you try, the waves keep coming. The solution is, to simply step back and sit on the beach. There you can watch the waves come and go. That is how you can be at peace.

Quiet professional

Elite members of the military all share some similar qualities. One of them is being a quiet professional. They are proven individuals who understand the big picture. The race in life is only against themselves. They never make excuses, but take responsibility for their actions. Every day they seek to get better. Quiet professionals do not speak more than what needs to be said because they let their actions do the talking. Be a quiet professional.

Learning

Learning is the acquisition of knowledge or skills through experience, study, or by being taught. Be a lifetime learner. All professionals have this common trait. Their ceiling for learning is extremely high. This leads to the ability to adapt. They continuously refine their ways and never think they know everything. [1]

Information not relevant to living is quickly forgotten. In the military, your life may be at risk. What you learn from training may be what saves you. Take what you are taught and extract the principle. Then, critically think about it. Lastly, apply what you learned in life. The last step is the most important. It is challenging and hard work. However, you can achieve a much higher level of understanding. Actively pursue knowledge.

The importance of learning

Learning brings a better overall understanding of life. It will make you more aware of your surroundings. An individual who is curious and learns is bound to have a more fulfilled life. It gives you exposure, understanding, and freedom to choose our own path.

Being an avid learner deepens your capacity to grow in all facets of life. These areas include awareness, understanding, knowledge, and skills. Some benefits for society are economic growth, understanding differences, and community health. If every person continually learns, it can help in the overall growth of humanity. [2]

Process of learning

The best place to start is by understanding what your learning style is. The different ways to learn are auditory (hearing), visual (seeing), kinesthetic (hands-on), or multi-sensory (a combination of the first three styles). Catering the subject matter to the way you learn best will not only make it easier but will have a lasting effect. [3]

Learning is closely related to problem-solving. Start by asking a question. Figure out what the answer is. Take what you found and think about *why* it is that way.

Understanding the *what* and *why* will lead to being able to think inside the specific subject matter.

A simple method to structured learning

You can learn anything. First, set realistic goals. This is a vital ingredient for success in anything you do. The goals need to be specific and tailored to exactly what you want to accomplish. If it is too difficult, procrastination may kick in. The task may become overwhelming.

On the other hand, you may get bored if it too easy. There needs to be a challenge. Secondly, have a time frame. Set a specific amount of time to accomplish your goal. This helps because you will know how long to focus on that topic. Having a clear end in sight will let you know how to pace yourself. Thirdly, you need to make time.

Discipline and persistence are key. Fourthly, keep learning after your goals are met.

Distractions

Physical pain can be associated with learning. A way to get around that is by turning off all distractions. Set a timer for twenty-five minutes. Focus on the subject matter as best as you can. After the timer goes off, take a break. This is helpful because the mind has two modes of learning. The different states are the focus and diffuse (resting) modes. You can learn during each mode. Understanding how to utilize both is important. In the end, do one thing at a time, be persistent, rest, and make sure you practice. [5]

Resources for learning

There are many ways to gather information. Know where your facts are coming from. Learn to filter good from bad sources. Make sure you can trust them. [4]

Ways to find information: Books, articles, magazines, journals, the internet, classes, podcasts, documentaries, observing your surroundings, and by a hands-on approach

Good sources: Academic journals, professional associations, government agencies, major news outlets, accredited schools

Bad sources: Blogs, web forums, untrusted random websites, severely biased news organizations, and peoples opinions or interpretations

Here is a sequence of learning:

1. Ask a specific question

2. Search

3. Screen

4. Digest

5. Synthesize

6. Use the information

7. Test what you know

8. Get feedback

9. Regulate

10. Refine

11. Maintain

Common techniques for learning:

- Memorizing

- Underlining

- Taking notes

- Mind mapping

- Flashcards

- Quizzes

- Brainstorming

- Mnemonic devices

- Organized studying

- Drawing

- Following an established learning program

- Talking to teachers, mentors, colleagues, or subject

  matter experts

- Taking a class online or in person

- Finding a curriculum, or syllabus, and making your

  plan based off of it

How I like to learn

I always viewed school as a pain. The reasons given for learning seemed irrelevant to me. That is until I began to question what was going on in this strange world. The biggest questions in life revealed to me that I did not know anything. To start figuring out what was going on around me, I researched how to learn. Today, I come up with a list of questions. Things I am curious about. The subjects always have a purpose for something I am doing. My process is short and sweet. I learn what I can and move on.

My strategy:

- Ask a specific question
- Use credible sources to learn what you seek. I personally like reading books, watching educational videos, going to short classes, attending events.
- Explaining to myself what I just learned
- Write a short paper. I keep all my documents so I can refresh myself on the topic in the future
- Teach someone about what I learned
- Have a discussion to challenge what I know
- Test myself a week later to see if I still remember what you learned
- Move to the next subject

ASVAB study format

Day 1 - Take a practice test. See what areas are your strongest and weakest.

Day 2-9 - Read the complete study guide. Study two sections a day. Take notes. After each chapter, talk out loud to yourself about everything you just read.

Day 10-14 - Reread all the subjects that you are weak at.

Day 15 -Teach someone what you learned from the study guide.

Day 16 - Rest.

Day 17 - Take a practice test. Assess how much you have progressed. Repeat from day 1 if necessary.

Family

Your family will be coming along for the ride while serving. It is crucial to stay close to them. Communicate with them any changes or struggles, they will understand you better. It is vital you regularly build these relationships. Failing to do so can cause a lot of stress. Having issues at home can seriously affect your work and vice versa.

Deployments and training cycles can be challenging on relationships. There needs to be sureness in the purpose. Contribute to them to keep them healthy. Everyone needs to be on the same page. It takes trust, respect, and an open communication line. Problems at home will only be amplified while you are deployed. You may not come home to a warm house, or even to a spouse. Take your family seriously, you need each other. No one can read your mind. You have to be able to talk when something is wrong. The more you open up, the closer the relationships will be. Everyone will benefit.

It may be hard to separate work from home. Your job requires you to be aggressive and destructive. At work, anger is commended. Acting the same way off duty will only cause problems. When you go home, you must act very different. There you are expected to be quiet, courteous, and polite. This polarizing expectation to instantly adapt may be extremely hard to deal with. Recognize what is being asked of you. Do your best to explain this to family. Doing so will really ease the tension.

Domestic abuse

Domestic abuse is a serious issue. If you can not control your emotions, then you absolutely need to seek help. Abusing another person is not ok, in any context. Recognize you are doing something destructive. Be humble and seek outside guidance. Getting help is a very admirable and mature act. No one will look down on you. People will only respect you for trying to better yourself.

No one is perfect. The only way to set yourself up for success is to start by recognizing that you have a problem. Then, be proactive and communicate your struggle. Finally, learn healthy ways to cope. Refine the process by receiving feedback from your family. It will take time, but it is incredibly worth it.

Rushed marriages

Do your best to avoid a rushed marriage. The rate of divorce is higher for military members than in the civilian world. The lifestyle is hugely taxing on relationships. Many people can not handle the stress. Getting married at the moment may seem great. That is until you learn your spouse took all your money while you were on deployment and left. Or when you find out your wife is three months pregnant, while you were on a six-month deployment. This does not happen to everyone, but it does happen. Take your time and choose the right partner.

Marriages can work while you are in the military. Expect it to be very hard. It is a serious decision and should be a thought out plan. Be able to separate momentary passion from a long term commitment. Infatuation is often mistaken for love. Even if the other person seems perfect, they are not, *and* neither are you. See the person as they really are.

Choose a lifelong partner. It needs to be a person you can establish a family with. Having kids while in the military comes with serious downsides. You will not be there for them like you will want to be. Being gone so much can be unfair to those kids. The best choice may be to wait until after you get out to start a family. If the military is a career for you, then you will have to accept the difficulties and do your best.

Drugs & supplements

Drugs

The Military does not tolerate illegal drug use in the slightest. Let's say a specific drug, like marijuana, is legal in the state you live. However, that same drug is still illegal federally. If you consume and get caught, you will be punished by the federal laws. Drug tests are a recurring task throughout your military career. There are significant consequences for being caught with an illegal substance. One possible repercussion can be getting booted out of the military with a dishonorable discharge. Take this stuff seriously if you really want to succeed. Ask yourself if the temporary high is worth the embarrassment and your job.

Supplements

You might walk into someone's barracks room and think you just walked into a supplement store. Supplements are highly used among military members. This is mainly due to the pressures from needing to perform and the desire to be strong. Be cautious of what you take. No one actually inspects what goes on the shelves at your local supplement store. They are not regulated by the government. The product you bought might be from a guy who picked "organic" plants off the side of a highway. The plants may be covered in chemicals from cars that drove by. Years ago, a popular pre-workout was banned from being sold on military bases. It was deemed illegal after several people died. The pre-workout had one ingredient that registered as an amphetamine. Be smart about what you put in your body.

Steroids

Steroids are a commonly used drug. They are illegal to take in the military. Although you can see substantial gains from taking steroids, there are many side effects of improper usage. If you are seriously considering this option, consult the medic in your platoon first. Learn the proper way to use this enhancer. Consider the risks before you start injecting yourself.

Supplements conclusion

Steroids and all other supplements are not actually necessary to be competent in the military. Sticking to a proper diet, regular exercise, and sleep are all you need. Taking a bunch of creatine will help you in the short term.

However, when you stop taking the supplement, you will either store what you put on as fat or lose everything. The more you take, the more you have to maintain. It comes at a cost.

Alcohol

Being in the military and drinking alcohol go hand in hand, they always have. Especially with the reality that you can die on your next deployment. It is illegal to drink under the age of twenty-one, even for military members. There can be consequences if you get caught drinking underage. In the end, the choice is yours. If you do not drink at all, be prepared for peer pressure.

Come up with a plan before you drink in public. Do your best to ensure you have a designated driver (D.D.). Be aware that the D.D. might drink anyway. Have a backup plan to call a taxi service or someone sober from your unit. If you fall asleep in your car because you are trying to do the right thing, you still might get a DUI. It is not worth getting kicked out of the military, and the money you will have to spend. The legal fees can be between ten to twenty thousand dollars.

The main ways people get in trouble with alcohol:

- Driving under the influence (DUI)
- Fighting
- Being drunk on duty
- Underage drinking

Medical records

A medical record is a physical folder that will store all personal health information. Your file will be created when you in-process at a Military Entrance Processing Station (MEPS). That same record follows you during your entire time in the military. To maximize your benefits aftward, make sure every single medical visit is documented. Doing so will provide a paper trail if you need to make a claim for healthcare or disability.

Everything should automatically be added to your file, but it is best to always double check. Visits for minor injuries or illnesses may not be added to your portfolio. Ask for a copy and put it in yourself. People do not disclose their injuries as often in the special operations community. Which means that not everything gets recorded. This mainly happens on deployment. Be on top of your game to help you and your family after you get out.

Money

The mindset of a military member may be one more of survival than longevity. As I mentioned at the beginning of the book, I never expected to come back from a deployment. That mentality followed me for a long time. Planning things a year ahead seemed pointless. In my mind, I could be dead at any moment. In reality, the chances are good that you will go back to living a normal life. With that in mind, you need to plan for the future.

Military members get paid twice a month. The pay scale is based on your rank and service time. Also, you will receive housing, food, medical care, and clothing (only military). You also have the option to contribute to a retirement fund and life insurance. On top of that, you may be entitled to receive a bonus when you sign up. A bonus depends on how desperate the military is at recruiting new people. That is when they offer incentives like money to sign up.

Many people who join the military do not come from homes with a lot of money. Gaining a secure income might even be why some join. People outside the military will know you have money coming in. Be careful, so you do not get taken advantage of.

Money provides the opportunity to buy things. The first thing many people do is go out and purchase an expensive car. It may be fun at first. However, if you can not pay back the loan you took out, that excitement will instantly disappear. When you try to resell that car, you will quickly learn it was a terrible investment. Buy durable things, items that you plan to keep for a long time.

Make a decision to be responsible with your money. There is a much better way to set yourself up for the long term. You can still have fun, just be smart with what you earn. Choose to save and invest. The earlier you start, the more you will have in the future. If you spend recklessly, you can get stuck in a lot of debt. Debt is like being in prison. Stay away from it as best as you can. If you put in a little effort, you can really set yourself up for success.

Bonus

Signing up may come with a bonus. Who does not want to get a large amount of cash for signing up? There is a catch. You can get a bonus if you qualify, commit, *and* you complete the contract you signed up for. Meaning, if you sign a four-year contract and receive a bonus, you have to stay in for four years to keep that money. Yes, Uncle Sam can give and take.

Re-enlisting may come with another bonus. Before you think about purchasing a fourth motorcycle, make sure you really want to stay in. There are many other ways to make money outside the military. Think before signing the re-enlistment paperwork. Have a good reason to stay in. You might regret it.

Budgeting

The goal is to live under your means. If you make two thousand dollars per month, try to spend only one thousand five hundred. Put the remaining money into a savings and investing account. Doing this can help you purchase big items like a house. It will also come in handy in the event of an emergency. Having a savings account, investing, and budgeting will really help cut down on stress as well. It is much easier to focus on the things you enjoy when you know your bills are covered. Being able to make money is a part of survival. Be smart with what you earn.

Retirement fund

Thrift Savings Plan (TSP) - is a retirement fund for military members. You can contribute a portion of your paycheck to your retirement fund. The money you set aside will eventually become an income for after you retire. Even if you put in a small amount per month, it is an excellent investment for your future.

Investing

Real estate - The value of a house typically goes up over time. There are three options for making money from real estate. First, sell the house when the cost is higher than when you bought it. Second, rent out the house. Third, fix up the property and sell it. There is a risk in buying real estate. Learn more before you purchase.

Stock market - Purchase small ownership in a large company. Investing in the stock market contributes to the global economy. You can make money by buying a stock and selling it above what you purchased. Another way is the company can give stockholders a dividend when they make a profit. Not all companies offer dividends. Do not trade in the stock market until you fully understand what is going on. Research each company you choose to invest in.

Roth IRA - This is an investment account. It is available at most banks. You can choose where to put your money or have the bank do it for you. A significant advantage of investing in this account is the tax breaks. Contact your bank to learn more about opening a Roth IRA.

Immigrants

The United States of America is a country built on immigrants. Non-citizens *can* join the military. In order to enlist, you have to be a *legal permanent immigrant*. However, there are restrictions. For example, you can not sign up to be an officer. Also, there are specific jobs you will not be allowed to do. These jobs require a security clearance. You will not be able to obtain a clearance until you receive your citizenship.

After you enlist, you can apply to become a citizen. The process is faster than if you apply as a civilian. Contact the local naturalization representative at the base you get stationed at, they will help you get started. [6]

Chapter 4 - Mental Health

PTSD

Post-traumatic stress disorder (PTSD) is when an event shocks you mentally and/or emotionally. A traumatizing experience may cause adverse changes in your brain. Many side effects can occur. Understanding what PTSD is, along with the right treatment, can help you recover from experiencing something painful. [1]

The general public has talked about PTSD since the terrorist attacks on September 11, 2001. However, it is not a new disorder. You do not have to be in the military to have experienced a scarring event. Going through something stressful can be traumatizing.

These intense situations can cause a person to struggle afterward. The effects may occur immediately or take years to show. For instance, a veteran hears fireworks in the distance. The explosions may remind him of losing his teammate from a roadside bomb during one of his deployments overseas. The result can cause depression and a change in his mood. This is an example of PTSD.

Another example is a marines base keeps getting hit by rockets. After he arrives home, he and his buddies go to a sporting event. A referee at the game uses his whistle. The marine physically braces for impact because the sound is a reminder of an incoming explosion. PTSD may cause some side effects without an individual realizing it. The symptoms or reactions will manifest in various ways for each person.

These internal changes can be healed. First, you have to analyze yourself. Look to see if deep down you are wounded. Secondly, figure out what triggers are causing the change. Thirdly, recognize what past experience may still be affecting you. Lastly, restructure that unpleasant memory to where you can live in peace. Accept that you can not change the past. Realize it may take years to recover. Working through these steps will make you stronger. The only person that can really help you is you.

General types and symptoms

Intrusive memories: [2]

- Thinking of a memory, you do not want to think of
- Having a flashback of a particular event

- Nightmares

- Having a physical or emotional reaction when something reminds you of an unpleasant experience

Avoidance:

- You go out of your way to avoid anything that reminds you of the event

- You do not like thinking or talking about what happened

Negative changes in thinking or mood:

- Contemplating or planning suicide

- Memory loss

- Fear of getting in close relationships

- You do not care for things you previously enjoyed

- It is hard to be happy or excited

- Being numb to your surroundings

- Distant from family and friends

Being extra sensitive physically and/or emotionally:

- Hypervigilance. Being really alert all the time

- Self-destructive behavior

- Problems sleeping

- Have an issue concentrating

- Irritable

- Anger outbursts

- Aggressive or threatening behavior

- Guilt or shame

- Feeling overwhelmed

Depression

Many factors can contribute to depression. The leading causes are from not having a purpose, a lack of close friends, struggling to cope with the past, or you have a chemical imbalance in your brain. Overcoming depression is difficult. The good news is that things can get better. Understanding what contributes to your depression is extremely important. Take a proactive approach to find the root cause. That information will guide the recovery process.

Suicide

Military members have a high risk of contemplating or committing suicide. It is an epidemic in the United States. Be honest with yourself. If you are thinking of taking your life, talk to someone you can trust. Discussing your struggles can help find the root of the cause. You are not weird or wrong for thinking these things. The only thing you can control is how you react to these thoughts.

Have a sound support system. You need to have people around that you can trust, where you have each other's backs. A place where you can freely share your problems. This will have a night and day effect on working through your issues. The hole will only get deeper if you keep everything to yourself. The struggle is real. Do not try to do things alone. There is strength in numbers.

The highest risk for suicide: [(3)]

- American (from a western developed country)

- White

- Male

- Have a gun (or access to one)

- Divorced

- Military member or veteran

My story with PTSD, depression, and suicide

I personally check all the boxes for being at high risk for suicide. Some of the lowest points in my life were the days after I got back from a deployment. The flight home was my transition time from combat missions to being at home. Preparing my gear for a mission one night. The next, I would be back stateside in my barracks room.

The first night back from overseas was always the worst. Guys with families left as quick as they could. I would take my bags and go sit in my room. Sitting in silence, I would contemplate taking my life. I felt empty and alone and did not know who to talk to. At least one of my buddies experienced the same thing. I am sure many more struggled, but no one ever talked about it. Alcohol was a band-aid. Time would pass, but the depression and struggle still remained.

After I got out of the military, I went back home and tried to resume life like it was before I joined. I did not think anything about PTSD, depression, or even suicide. In my mind, I thought I had dealt with everything appropriately and would not have an issue.

My own understanding of PTSD was almost none. I thought the disorder meant that a disturbed person would have violent nightmares. Their issues would possibly lead to shooting up a public place. This is a common view of PTSD. However, it is much more than that. For me, I started to become detached. Without reason, I would be depressed, anxious, angry, and irritable. My lows would last for days or even weeks. I did not realize I had an issue because I thought my mood swings were typical. As it turns out, this is *not* normal.

In public areas, I would play out what I would do if an active shooter came into the room. My mind would get so exhausted from hypervigilance. I could not really rest anywhere but in my room. When people would slam doors, I would freeze inside because I thought it was a rocket coming in. I would distrust people if I sensed they did not have my back. That situation was equivalent to room clearing. If someone does not cover your back clearing a compound, it could mean your life.

My mind was still stuck in combat. I would sit in silence, waiting for chaos and explosions. In the distance at times, I swore I heard machine guns. People around would say different. I would need to know the plan. In my mind, if you did not think things out, someone could get killed. People who have not been in combat will not understand why I would think like this.

All of these small things added up and really took away from living a more "normal" life. It severely affected and destroyed my marriage. The other person did not even try to understand what I was going through. I did my best to communicate what I knew. Ultimately, it did not really matter. I was told I used PTSD as an excuse. This was after I was diagnosed with it. That same person's dream was to help veterans and people... with PTSD. The reason I share this story is to show you how distant the understanding is of those who were in combat, compared to those who have no clue what that means.

All of your issues will be magnified in a lousy environment. You need to receive love, care, space, and understanding. During my marriage, I suffered a lot. I lost a lot of weight, struggled to focus on work, could not see the future, had several anxiety attacks, went through depressions, and had intrusive thoughts that were destructive. Many things factored into the destruction of my marriage. I know that I am solely responsible for my actions and contributions to what happened. However, PTSD did contribute to the chaos.

Ways to get help

It starts by realizing you are struggling. Recognize if you have PTSD, are depressed, or have had suicidal ideation. You need to help yourself before others can help you. Be honest about your struggles with someone you trust. Most people think therapy is just sitting on a couch, talking about their feelings. It can be difficult trusting a stranger with your thoughts. The fear of judgment or shame can cause a limit on how much you say. For some people that works, but that approach may not be for you. The good news is there are many other outlets available to help clear your mind. The goal is to get away from destructive thoughts and find a purpose for the future. You need to see that life moves on. Find something that works best for you.

Different forms of therapy:

- Counseling. Individual or group

- Occupational therapy. Pick any activity you enjoy. The therapist will integrate therapy into that activity. It can be verbal or non-verbal

- Nature. Hiking, camping, fishing, hunting, or even sitting in a forest

- Exercise. Running, biking, swimming, lifting

- Sports. Baseball, basketball, football, snowboarding, surfing, etc

- Volunteering. Veterans in need, homeless, children

- Meditation

Mental health conclusion

The issues in the story I just shared with you still affect me today. However, I have challenged my struggles and have been seeking to learn what is really going on. I have been able to articulate my thoughts and share the root issues. Before, I would get stuck on a surface level problem that only went in circles. With time, I have been able to progress and get better. You can do the same.

Learn from my story. Assess yourself to see where you are. See how you are contributing when things spiral. You can not control anyone else but yourself. Any traumatic issue will change you. It is nothing to be ashamed of. There are people out there who do care and will hear you. Those who do not even try to understand are not worth your time.

During your life, you may struggle. There may be times when you feel isolated, depressed, and/or lost. Prepare yourself now, knowledge is power. Understand what is happening and learn how to deal with it. This is the best way to set yourself up to fight hard times.

Only you can actually understand what you went through. It was your experience. No other person can know the effect a situation has on you. If you want someone to understand, communicate your feelings with them. Opening up to another person will build an emotional bridge. It will help you both understand each other better. The result will be a deep and lasting bond.

The future can be brighter. Any issues you have can be understood and conquered. PTSD and depression can be fought and dealt with. The thoughts or attempts at suicide can be left in the past. Choose your purpose and do not stray from it. Find your tribe and give them everything you have. There you will find your place. You are not alone. Fight for a better tomorrow.

If you are seriously considering suicide, and have no one to talk to, call the veteran suicide prevention line anytime.

Call - 1-800-273-8255 and press 1

Text - 838255

Chapter 5 - The United States Military

The United States of America is a federal republic based on a constitution. It is comprised of fifty different states and several territories. The U.S. Constitution was written in 1787. It is the written document that our government is based on. Federal means that the power of the nation is divided between one central government and each state's own administration. A republic implies that the representatives in the office were elected by the people.

A nation is essentially a vast tribe. This group needs protection from outside threats. The sole purpose of the military is to fight for the belief system they are founded on. The members of the armed forces are the tribes' people who have decided to be the protectors.

Past battles were fought with bows and spears. Today we fly jets, get launched from submarines, jump out of airplanes, and sprint off helicopters to fight our enemies. That is just to name a few of the modern day warfare advancements.

Several departments make up the U.S. military. The need to fight in specific ways is the reason why there are numerous branches. The Air Force is a split off from the Army because the demand was too much for one branch to cover warfare on land and in the air. It is slowly but continuously changing. In the future, another branch will be established called the Space Force. You may think that means fighting aliens with laser guns. I wish you were right. In reality, it has to do with satellites, security, and spying.

Military members can work in designated areas on the planet. The Active Duty and Reserve components work for the federal government. Their area of responsibilities is outside the United States border. The members in the National Guard work for the specific state they signed up in. They can conduct military operations inside and outside the United States.

Chain of command [1]

Executive Branch

Commander in Chief - The President is the head of the state and federal government. They lead the executive branch and serves as the Commander and Chief of the worlds largest military.

Department of Defense

<u>Secretary of Defense</u> - They are the leader of the United States Department of Defense. They are second in command of the U.S. military, after the President.

<u>Chairman of the Joint Chief of Staff</u> - This person is the highest ranking officer in the United States military. They are an aide for the President and the Secretary of Defense in making decisions. The Chairman advises them on what actions they can or can not take. By law, this position does not have direct authority in commanding the armed forces.

Military departments

Army - Primary ground force in the event of a conflict or war. It was founded on June 14, 1775. Currently, there is around one million uniformed personnel. This number includes the National Guard and Reserve. It is the oldest branch in American history. The Army has fought in every major battle the U.S. has partaken in. [2]

Army Special Operations

75th Ranger Regiment: [3]

- Name: Rangers
- Purpose: Light infantry, door kickers

- Primary mission: Airfield seizure, direct action

- Date established: 1974

- GT score: 105

- Selection: Ranger Assessment and Selection Process (RASP) - 8 weeks

- Additional: Airborne and Ranger School. (Ranger School is a leadership school you have to complete if you want to become a non-commissioned officer in Ranger battalion. It is essentially a rite of passage.)

Special Forces: [4]

- Name: SF

- Purpose: Teachers

- Primary mission: Unconventional warfare, force multipliers

- Date established: 1952

- GT score: 110

- Selection: Special Forces Assessment Selection (SFAS) - 4 weeks

- Pipeline: Special Forces Qualification Course (Q course) - 12-18 months (MOS dependant)

160th Special Operations Aviation Regiment: [5]

- Name: Night Stalkers

- Purpose: Helicopter crew

- Primary mission: Transport troops by air

- Date established: 1981

- GT score: 100

- Selection: Fill out paperwork and apply

- Pipeline: Basic NightStalker Course - 5 weeks

- Training Cycle: Basic Mission Qualified to Fully Mission Qualified - 3 years

- Additional: You have to already be in the military to apply.

<u>Navy:</u> Water-based defense and offense of the United States. It was established on October 13, 1775. There are around half a million uniformed members. It is the largest and most capable navy on the planet. The size of the U.S. Navy is a combination of the next thirteen countries naval force. The Navy has a global presence with major defense capabilities and readiness. [6]

Navy Special Operations

<u>Sea, Air, and Land Teams:</u> [7]

- Name: SEALS
- Purpose: Special water operations, direct action, force multipliers
- Primary mission: Unconventional warfare by water
- Date established: 1962
- GT score:110

- Selection: Basic Underwater Demolition School (BUDS) - 24 weeks

- Pipeline: SEAL Qualification Training (SQT) - 26 weeks

Special Warfare Combatant-craft Crewmen: [8]

- Name: SWCC

- Purpose: Boat teams with large guns

- Primary mission: Transport SEALS and other troops via small boats

- Date established: 1987

- GT score: 100

- Selection: Special Warfare Combatant-Craft Crewmen Indoctrination - 3 weeks

- Pipeline: SWCC Basic Crewman Training - 7 weeks

- Name: EOD

- Purpose: Explosive experts who can dive and
  HALO

- Primary mission: Dispose of explosives

- Date established: 1941

- GT score: 110

- Selection: EOD Prep Course of Instruction - 3
  weeks

- Pipeline: Basic EOD Dive School, Basic EOD
  Training, Airborne, EOD Tactical Training - 51
  weeks

Marines: To be a bridge from water to land, in the event of
a large scale war. It was founded on November 10, 1775.
The Marines fall under the umbrella of the Navy since June
30, 1834. There are around a quarter million marines. They
primarily perform amphibious operations. They are also

used as a rapid deployment force. Marines also have a presence at United States embassies across the world. [10]

Marines Special Operations

Marine Special Operations Command: [11]

- Name: MARSOC, Raiders

- Purpose: Teachers, intelligence gathering

- Primary mission: Reconnaissance, force multipliers, unconventional warfare

- Date established: 2006

- GT score: 105

- Selection: Assessment and Selection 1 & 2 (A&S) - 6 weeks

- Pipeline: Individual Training Course (ITC) - 9 months

- Additional: Must be in for three years before you can try out.

Air Force: Air and space-based defense and offense of the United States. It was founded on August 1, 1907. There are around half a million members. Primarily, they provide air support in combat. They also transport the other branches around via planes. It is the largest and most technologically advanced air force in the world. [12]

Air Force Special Operations

Combat Controller: [13]

- Name: CCT
- Purpose: Calls in air strikes, set up aircraft landings
- Primary mission: Air traffic controller
- Date established: 1953

- Specific CCT test: 30 (minimum)

- Selection: Air Force Combat Control Selection Course - 2 weeks

- Pipeline: Combat Control Operator Course, Combat Control School - 29 weeks

Pararescuemen: [14]

- Name: PJs

- Purpose: Medics who can HALO and scuba

- Primary mission: Combat search and rescue (CSAR)

- Date established: 1946

- ASVAB: 44 (minimum)

- Pipeline: Air Force Pararescue Indoctrination Course - 8 weeks

- Pipeline: Air Force Pararescue Recovery Specialist course - 24 weeks

- Additional: Airborne, Diver School, HALO, medical courses

Joint Special Operations Command (JSOC): These are the special mission units (SMU). You need to be in the military for several years before you can apply for these units. They are all challenging to get into. They can conduct very specific operations. Each group is exceptionally professional and consists of the best men and women in the military. [15]

JSOC units

Delta Force - They become whatever is needed

75th Ranger Regiment's - Regimental Reconnaissance Company - Reconnaissance and intelligence

SEAL Team 6 - Unconventional warfare, hostage rescue

<u>24th Special Tactics Squadron</u> - Comprised of Combat Controllers, Special Operations Weather Technicians, Pararescuemen, and Tactical Air Control Party

<u>Intelligence Support Activity</u> - Intelligence gathering

Chapter 6 - Enlisting

<u>Step 1</u> - Decide to join

First, you have to decide that you want to join the military. Next, choose which branch to sign up for. Lastly, pick the job you would like to do. Have a couple of jobs in mind in case your first choice is not available. The military offers many jobs. A few examples are infantryman, mechanic, and firefighter. The Army alone provides over one hundred and fifty jobs. Once you get into the military, you *can* transfer to another job. However, it takes time. You will have to go back through Advanced Individual Training (AIT).

<u>Step 2</u> - Contact a recruiter

After you decide what you want to do, contact a local recruiter. Learn as much as you can before signing any paperwork. Some recruiters may sign you up for things you do not really want, so be careful. Make sure you get everything written down on paper (*this is very important*). If not, the details could change without you realizing it. You will need to come to an agreement on terms like contract length, the job you will do, and incentives. Several incentives you may qualify for are being guaranteed a military school or receiving a money bonus. Once you agree on these terms, you will begin doing paperwork.

<u>Step 3</u> - Gather paperwork

The next part of the process is gathering all the paperwork your recruiter asks for. You will have to provide a lot of information about yourself. For example, where you have lived in the past or if you have been to prison. There are things you may write down that can disqualify you. Explain any issues you have with your recruiter. Depending on the situation, a recruiter may fill out a waiver. This will allow you to sign up, even with a disqualifier.

Keep the personal information you provide the same throughout your military career. In the future, you may need to fill out similar paperwork to receive a security clearance. You might have issues if the information does not match your previous paperwork. Answer only what they ask you and stay consistent.

<u>Step 4</u> - MEPS

The Military Entrance Processing Station (MEPS) is a government building where you will officially sign your contract to join the military. Your medical portfolio will also be created. The process takes two long days. Each day you will sit in a lobby doing various exams. The results show if you qualify to join or not. Some of the tests conducted are an eye exam, weight measurement, and general flexibility.

Each branch has a specific standard you need to be within. Airborne School recruits will have an additional physical. The results from your exam *may* disqualify you from the military or for a specific job. For example, if you are color blind, you may not be allowed to become a pilot.

The people working there may treat you like a private. At this point in the process, you are not in the military. Just make sure to be respectful. The employees may have a short temper because they deal with new recruits and the same problems every single day. Be patient. Do not be in a rush. Play the game and get it over with.

A large part of the MEPS process will be the Armed Services Vocational Aptitude Battery (ASVAB). This test is a basic version of the American College Test (ACT) or Scholastic Assessment Test (SAT) given in high school. The topics covered are general science, arithmetic reasoning, word knowledge, paragraph comprehension, mathematics knowledge, and electronics information.

The results of this test determine what jobs you are eligible for. Higher scores offer more opportunities. The test is at your own pace. It usually takes several hours to complete. If you score low, you can retake it after a certain period. Prepare beforehand. For a recommended study guide, go to PreCombatCheck.com or MARCH2SUCCESS.com.

Step 5 - Swear in

After two long days of testing and paperwork, you will finally be done with your *initial* in-processing. Before you swear in, you will know what your military job will be, how long your contract is, and if you are getting a bonus. Shortly after completing everything, a ceremony will be conducted. This is where you will be sworn in by an officer. Your family can come and see you during this time.

Immediately after you swear in, you will sign your contract. Congratulations, you have *officially* enlisted. You are now a member of the United States Armed Forces.

Step 6 - Ship out to boot camp

Boot camp is where your military career begins. Those who sign up for the Active Duty will be put on a plane following MEPS. They will be sent to wherever their boot camp is. Whatever personal items are brought to MEPS will be taken to basic training. The National Guard or Reserve recruits may have a delayed entry before starting boot camp.

Drill sergeants will greet you the day you arrive (or drill instructors for some branches). This is where you will say goodbye to your hair. You will begin doing more paperwork and issued all your gear. Here is where you will be taught how to march in formation. Prepare to do push-ups and wait in long lines to eat food.

You will get everything issued for your time in the military. Some things you will receive are your military ID, uniforms, boots, duffel bags, and socks. Make sure you keep all of your issued items. You will have to turn in just about everything they give you. Anything lost will be paid from your pocket.

In-processing can take one to four weeks. It just depends on how many people are there waiting to receive their gear. Personally, I thought the in-processing was worse than basic training. From there, you will be assigned to your basic training unit. That is when you will begin training to become a Soldier, Marine, Seaman, or Airman.

Chapter 7 - Recruiter Q & A

I sent an email to an Army recruiter with these basic entry level questions. Here are his answers:

<u>What is MEPS?</u> - Military Entrance Processing Station. It is where you will get a medical examination, do paperwork, and sign your enlistment contract to join the military. It typically takes two days to in-process before you get shipped to boot camp.

<u>What is the ASVAB?</u> - Armed Services Vocational Aptitude Battery is a multiple choice test administered by the United States Military Entrance Processing Command. The scores are used to determine qualification for enlistment in the United States Armed Forces.

How do you get the job you want? - Military Occupational Specialty (MOS), also known as your job. The selection is based on the ASVAB test results.

How can you study for it? - You can use MARCH2SUCCESS.com, which is the only study material that the Army sponsors.

What happens if you fail? - If you fail, you have to wait thirty calendar days before a retest can be administered.

Can family come to MEPS when you swear in? - Yes, family members are allowed to be present for the swear-ins.

What is the difference between enlisted and officer? - Officers have their bachelor degrees. They have different responsibilities versus enlisted soldiers. Officers can lead at a high level, as well as fly aircraft. Enlisted personnel start at the lowest ranks.

What jobs can I do in the military? - There are over one hundred and fifty jobs in the United States Army. Your ASVAB test scores determine what jobs are available to you.

Do you get paid while in the military? - Yes, you get paid on the first and fifteenth of every month. The pay scale is based on your rank and time served.

What benefits are you entitled to? - Low cost to free medical, dental, tuition assistance, and the Montgomery GI Bill (for school).

Is there a bonus if you sign up? - If you qualify for a bonus and if there is a bonus available.

What are the contract lengths you can sign up for? - Three to five years. However, regardless of the length of the contract, there is an eight-year obligation. It means if you sign a four-year contract, you still owe the military four years in the Individual Ready Reserve (IRR). Being in the IRR means if a war broke out, they can call you and put you back in Active Duty or the Reserves. You are already trained. It makes adding people quicker and more cost effective. During your IRR time, you do not have to show up anywhere, train, or do anything.

Can a person try out for a special operations unit right off the street? - Yes, you can go into the 18X program (Special Forces) or get a Ranger contract. There are specific requirements you must meet to enlist into these programs.

What if a person signs up and changes their mind, can they leave the military? - It is possible. However, once you serve, your military records follow you for the rest of your life.

What happens if a person gets injured while serving? - You will receive a limited duty profile. This will allow you time to recover from your injury. Depending on the injury, you may have to attend physical therapy. You can also claim that injury for disability rating by going through the Veterans Affair (VA) upon leaving the military.

Can my spouse come with me when I get assigned to my duty station? - Yes, your spouse can go with you to your duty station. However, this is only after the completion of Basic Training and Advanced Individual Training (school for your job).

Chapter 8 - Getting Out

The military's way of saying you are getting out is called "expiration-term of service" (ETS). This means you are leaving the military. Getting out is a transition process every single person handles differently.

Learn all the information needed to best help you make the transition easier. I literally had twelve days to turn my things in and leave. I missed out on a lot of information because of it. Years have passed since my service time, and I am still learning about the benefits I qualify for.

There is a checklist of things you need to do before you are released. Try not to just go through the motions. Take advantage of the information given. It will really help you in the long run. The most important thing I suggest is getting your medical records updated. Then, talk to someone from the VA. This will best help you get set up for life after you leave the service. If not, you may have an uphill battle to fight. You will have issues getting medical care from the VA if you do not have paperwork.

Mental Transition

The most challenging part of getting out is the mental transition. If you are not prepared to accept the change, you might find it hard to reintegrate back into society. The civilian world may leave you lost and frustrated. If you feel not understood, it is ok, you are not alone. Over time you can find your footing and begin a new path in life.

This is a transitionary period for you *and* your family. Seek help if you need it. Talk to someone if you are struggling. Having trustworthy people around during this time of change is *extremely* important. Do not try to do this alone. They may not understand what you are going through until you tell them.

Sit down and talk with them. Listen to what concerns and expectations they have of you. After that, express your issues and expectations of them. Having this simple conversation will make a world of difference. It will be easier for everyone involved. If you can not talk to family or friends, the place that can help is the VA or a VET center.

Many civilians have a hard time understanding veterans. This especially true for combat veterans. People who have never been in the military are incredibly distant from war. They have never experienced anything like it. The closest they have come is from watching movies or reading books. Military people see life very different than civilians.

War experiences come with a real struggle for survival. The need to fight to stay alive causes immense stress. Being in a firefight gives you a reality check. You will realize that you can die in an instant. You will have a much deeper understanding of human limits and life itself. That difference in perspective may be why the transition for veterans returning home can be so challenging.

Expect the change to be difficult. The goal is to reintegrate as best as you can. Some things may work against your transition. For example, deploying overseas as a security contractor. Going to the same countries as you did during your military time may keep your mind in the survival mindset. That connection can cause a delay in a full transition back to a "normal" life.

That was an issue that I personally went through. Contracting overseas made my transition difficult. I made a deliberate decision to quit and move forward. The process for everyone is different. Recognize what is holding you back. You have to choose to close that chapter and *decide* to start a new one. Make sure your expectations are realistic. The change will take time.

Purpose

Finding purpose after you get out may be stressful. In the military, your mission was given. There was a clear objective. In the civilian world, you have to make up your own purpose.

Pursue any dream you want. Being in the military will give you a solid foundation to build from. You will be organized and disciplined. Use what you learn to succeed as a veteran. Start by thinking about what you want to do in life. Write out your goals and make a plan. Focus solely on your chosen objective.

The most common thing I hear people miss from their military time is the camaraderie. You belonged to something awesome. In most cases, you will never be able to have that same level of trust. Ordinary life does not come with the excitement of firefights, rockets, or any other intense events.

Dependency on other people is required in wartime. In the civilian world, there is no need to rely on another person for safety. In combat, you share many hard moments with your buddies because you fight for each other. Confidence is gained when you know someone has your back. That ultimate trust creates a lifelong bond. It is difficult to find this level of trust in the civilian world.

Examples of groups (tribes) to join:

- Where you work
- Hunting groups
- Sports teams and leagues
- Local Gyms
- Martial arts (Brazilian jiu-jitsu, boxing, mixed martial arts)
- Specific groups that meet for topics like physics, beer, sports, art, etc
- Shooting ranges

- Buddies who also got out of the military

- Church

Ways to make your transition period easier:

- Expect there to be change

- Expect it to take time

- Expect never to do the exact same cool things you did in the military

- Stay close to your family. Let them know if you are having a hard time

- Have your own creed

- Focus on your chosen purpose

Work following the military

The last thing on your mind may be what life will be like when you get out. Your military career will end at some point. Unless you die during your service period, you will have to deal with adjusting back to being a civilian. It will take time to adapt no matter what you do.

A typical civilian job is a daily grind. The tasks may be easy and extremely repetitive. It may seem like there is no end in sight. The approach to leadership can be severely different. In the military, a senior officer can yell at someone to accomplish a task. There are consequences for those who do not listen. A typical punishment is doing a physical exercise like push-ups. Do that at your civilian job, and you most likely will be fired. Understanding the differences in culture will take time.

Have a plan for where you want to work when you get out. Make a list of the jobs you are interested in. Learn about those industries. Let's say you could see yourself becoming a firefighter. The first step is to go visit a fire station and ask to do a ride-along. If you do not feel good about that job, then move on to the next. If you are interested, then ask for more information.

The jobs most people see as closely relating to the military are government agency work, law enforcement, fire fighting, and security contracting. The reality is that even these jobs are not exactly the same as what you did in the military, especially if you were in a special operations unit. Working as a civilian comes with a lot more bureaucracy. The dynamics are just not the same.

Security contracting is a popular choice. The job is halfway from being a civilian to the military. These gigs typically pay well. It also allows for a lot of freedom.

However, from personal experience, the work is very unfulfilling. You put your life on pause to go overseas. There you willingly put yourself back in harm's way. It is difficult to progress at home if you do this job. There is a sense of patriotism that comes with deploying overseas. However, the main reason people do this job is for money. Many people get stuck because they get comfortable and have no plan to stop. Although you are around veterans, people will not have your back as they did in the military.

No job will be the same as your military service. One of my friends had to accept that he will never ride a helicopter onto a target again. That no matter what he does, nothing will be as exciting. This personal recognition allowed him to move forward because his priorities shifted. His purpose came from being with his family. Find fulfillment in your job.

School

Another option is to go to school. Most veterans qualify for a benefit called the G.I. Bill. This benefit will cover the cost to get a college degree. This is an excellent option if you are trying to figure out what you want to do in life.

Know what you want before starting. This will help you pick the right field of study. Realize that a college degree does *not* guarantee you a job. The best opportunities come from networking. It is about who you know, not what you know.

Start your own business

A great way to use all the skills you learned is by starting your own business. There are a lot of benefits offered to veterans who start their own businesses. For example, there is a program called Boots to Business. They help veterans transition from the military to starting a business. If you choose this route, you will have a lot of freedom and flexibility. Setting up a business online can allow you to travel while you make money. More time can be spent with family because you are the boss. There are many positives.

Running your own business provides the opportunity to generate your own income. Working for someone else will have a limit on how much money you can make. This route opens up a much higher ceiling for growth.

Starting a company can also contribute to your community. You can enrich people's lives with your services and/or products. If your business grows large enough, you can hire employees. With your earnings, you can contribute to different charities. Good things can come from something you build.

Working on your own can be very challenging. Initially, everything has to be done by you. Having a good plan does not guarantee you will make money. Most businesses do not see a profit until several years after they start. On top of that, many startup companies fail. It takes hard work and resilience to succeed. This route may be challenging but is highly recommended.

Benefits

There are many benefits that veterans are entitled to. The problem is that most do not know what is available. The government organization that handles the federal benefits is called the VA. The VA offers health care and many services for veterans. Also, each state may offer their own perks for those who served. Learn what you are entitled to. Take the time to do some research. It will help you and your family for the rest of your life. Make this a priority.

Common benefits veterans are entitled to

Health care - The VA provides health care for veterans. If you get sick, you can receive low-cost or free care at a VA hospital. Lifetime care is provided if you have a service-connected disability of ten percent or more. The only service they do not cover is dental care unless you are one hundred percent disabled. All veterans can apply online to see what they qualify for.

www.va.gov/health

Disability and compensation - Compensation can be given if you are injured during your service time. The injury must limit your ability to function normally. Disabilities can be mental or physical. Make sure all of your medical visits get documented. This will provide evidence supporting your claim. The process to receive compensation can take time. Back pay will be given for however long you wait if your claim is approved. Everything must be done through the VA.

www.ebenefits.va.gov/ebenefits/homepage

Boots to Business - This program is for veterans who want to start a business. They offer courses and provide many resources. Use this benefit to help make your idea a reality.

www.sba.gov/offices/headquarters/ovbd/resources/16051

G.I. Bill - This benefit helps veterans go back to school. Serve in the military for over three years, and your college fees will be covered. You will also receive a monthly check. Use this benefit to transition to another career field of your choice.

www.benefits.va.gov/gibill/docs/pamphlets/ch33_pamphlet. pdf

Vocational rehabilitation (Voc Rehab) - This benefit helps disabled veterans start a new career path. You need to have at least a thirty percent disability rating (ten percent, with a waiver) through the VA to qualify. The difference between this and the G.I. Bill is that you have to create a specific plan. A counselor must approve your path before you can start. This benefit can be used in addition to the G.I. Bill if you qualify.

www.benefits.va.gov/vocrehab/index.asp

VA house loan - This benefit is to help veterans purchase a house. There is no down payment necessary, and the interest rate will be low. You can use this benefit to invest in real estate. Not all homes for sale will accept a VA loan. When you talk to a real estate agent, let them know you plan to use this benefit. Contact the VA to receive the proper paperwork.

www.benefits.va.gov/homeloans/index.asp

For more information on benefits

benefits.va.gov/benefits

Conclusion

Do what is best for you and your family. Know what you want in life. Learn about all the options you have. Make a solid decision and commit to your choice. Realize that nothing is guaranteed. If you do not make it because you were not selected, or you were medically dropped, then walk away with your head held high. The only thing you can do is give everything you have.

You can be a beast no matter what you choose to do. Stay true to your creed. Live centered on principles, belong to a tribe, live out your core values, contribute to your relationships, and focus on your goals. You can accomplish great things. Nothing will be able to shake you. Screw playing it safe. Seek the fight.

I hope you learned a lot from reading this book. Now, go out there and crush life. *'Merica.* It really is the greatest country in the world.

For more information on signing up, go to PreCombatCheck.com. Listen to the PreCombat Check podcast on iTunes. Hear from veterans who were actually there.

Workout Plan

Here are a few ways you can structure your workout. This is simply to help get you started. Once you have specific goals, tailor your workouts to that target.

Keys to success

- Be consistent and bring intensity

- Lifting weights improperly can cause severe injuries. Proper form is paramount

- Shock your body, so it is forced to grow

- Always work out your core

- If you are trying to get strong, you need to use heavy weights

PT booster

Run improvement

<u>5-10 sets</u> - 30 seconds sprint, 60 seconds walk

<u>5-10 sets</u> - 60 seconds sprint, 120 seconds walk or jog

- Each week do 1 more set until you get to 10
- Once you can do 10 sets sprinting 30 seconds, then sprint for 60 seconds

The pyramid

<u>10 sets</u> - 1 pull-up, 2 push-ups, 3 sit-ups

- For each additional set, do 1 more pull-up, 2 more push-ups, and 3 more sit-ups. For example:
    - Set 1 - 1 pull-up, 2 push-ups, 3 sit-ups
    - Set 2 - 2 pull-ups, 4 push-ups, 6 sit-ups
    - Set 10 - 10 pull-up, 20 push-ups, 30 sit-ups
- Do not rest in between sets
- Do as many as you can until you reach muscle failure
- Muscle failure is *key*. When you are shaking and are about to collapse, that is where your body gets shocked and rebuilds the most
- To complete the pyramid, go up to 10 sets, and then come back down to 1

Military rucking shape

<u>Day 1</u> - Ruck - 5 miles (do *not* run). Every week aim to shave off five minutes off of your time

<u>Day 2</u> - PT Booster

<u>Day 3</u> - 5-mile run (timed)

<u>Day 4</u> - PT Booster

<u>Day 5</u> - Ruck a trail for 2 - 3 hours for a distance

-ALTERNATIVE-

<u>Day 1</u> - Ruck - 5 miles (do *not* run). Every week aim to shave off five minutes off of your time

<u>Day 2</u> - PT Booster

<u>Day 3</u> - Active recovery

<u>Day 4</u> - Ruck a trail for 2 - 3 hours for a distance

<u>Day 5</u> - PT Booster

Basic lifting format

<u>4 sets</u> - 10 repetitions per exercise

<u>Monday/Thursday</u> - Chest, shoulders, triceps

<u>Wednesday</u> - Run

<u>Tuesday/Friday</u> - Legs, back, biceps

<u>Saturday</u> - Run

-ALTERNATIVE-

<u>Day 1</u> - Chest, triceps

<u>Day 2</u> - Legs, shoulders

<u>Day 3</u> - Back, biceps

<u>Day 4</u> - Cardio

<u>Day 5</u> - Rest

<u>Day 6</u> - Repeat the first day

Lifting - 5X5s

All the information you need to do the 5x5 workout routine -

Stronglifts.com

<u>5 Sets</u> - 5 reps x each exercise

- Exercises are squat, bench press, deadlift, bent-over row, and shoulder press
- Each workout session, add 5 pounds total, to each exercise
- Start with very little weight
- Alternate week 1 and 2

Week 1

<u>Monday</u> - Squat, bench, bent-over rows

<u>Wednesday</u> - Squat, shoulder press, deadlift

<u>Friday</u> - Squat, bench, bent-over rows

Week 2

<u>Monday</u> - Squat, shoulder press, deadlift

<u>Wednesday</u> - Squat, bench, bent-over rows

<u>Friday</u> - Squat, shoulder press, deadlift

Military PFT Standards

Army

https://usarmybasic.com/army-physical-fitness/apft-standards

Navy

http://www.navy-prt.com/malestandard/malestandard.htm

Marines

https://www.military.com/military-fitness/marine-corps-fitness-requirements/usmc-physical-fitness-test

Air Force

https://airforce-pt.com/standards/air-force-pt-standards-male/air-force-fitness-standards-males-under-30/

Sources

Chapter 1 - Becoming a Warrior

1. Audie Murphy's Medal of Honor citation. Retrieved from National Museum of American History: https://americanhistory.si.edu/collections/search/object/nmah_1062079

2. Audie Murphy's quote. Retrieved from Wikipedia: https://en.wikipedia.org/wiki/Audie_Murphy#cite_note-86

3. The Ranger Creed. Retrieved from the Army: https://www.goarmy.com/ranger/about-the-rangers/ranger-creed.html

Chapter 2 - Strength

1. The myth of 1g/lb: Optimal protein intake. Retrieved from Science to Master your Physique by Menho Henselmans:

https://mennohenselmans.com/the-myth-of-1glb-optimal-protein-intake-for-bodybuilders/

2. What fats are. Retrieved from WebMD: https://www.webmd.com/diabetes/qa/what-are-fats

3. What Carbohydrates are. Retrieved from Wisegeek: https://www.wisegeek.com/what-are-carbohydrates.htm

4. Dehydration effects on the human body. Retrieved from Baptist health:https://share.baptisthealth.com/dehydration-effects-the-human-body/

5. How to catch up on sleep. Retrieved from Time: http://time.com/5541101/how-to-catch-up-on-sleep/

6. Circadian rhythm. Retrieved from Science daily: https://www.sciencedaily.com/terms/circadian_rhythm.htm

7. The four stages of a sleep cycle. Retrieved from Very well health: https://www.verywell.com/the-four-stages-of-sleep-2795920

Chapter 3 - Tips for Success

1. The definition of learning. Retrieved by Oxford Dictionaries: https://en.oxforddictionaries.com/definition/learning

2. How to study and learn. Retrieved from Critical thinking: http://www.criticalthinking.org/pages/how-to-study-and-learn-part-one/513

3. The learning process. Retrieved from Context Institute: http://www.context.org/iclib/ic06/gilman3/

4. Learn any subject. Retrieved from Wikihow: http://www.wikihow.com/Learn-Any-Subject-Without-Teachers

5. Learning how to learn. Retrieved from The Psychology Podcast: Learning how to learn with Barbara Oakley

6. Naturalized citizenship. Retrieved from Military hub: https://www.militaryhub.com/article?id=298, https://www.military.com/join-armed-forces/eligibility-requirements/the-us-military-helps-naturlize-non-citizens.html

Chapter 4 - Mental Health

1. PTSD definition. Retrieved from Oxford Dictionary: https://en.oxforddictionaries.com/definition/post-trau matic_stress_disorder

2. PTSD symptoms. Retrieved from Mayoclinic: https://www.mayoclinic.org/diseases-conditions/pos t-traumatic-stress-disorder/symptoms-causes/syc-2 0355967

3. Suicide statistics. Retrieved from American Foundation for Suicide Prevention: https://afsp.org/about-suicide/suicide-statistics/

Chapter 5 - United States Military

1. U.S. military breakdown. Retrieved from Wikipedia: https://en.wikipedia.org/wiki/Structure_of_the_Unite d_States_Armed_Forces

2. The Army definition. Retrieved from the Army: GoArmy.com

3. 75th Ranger Regiment. Retrieved from the Army: https://www.goarmy.com/ranger.html

4. Special Forces. Retrieved from the Army: https://www.goarmy.com/special-forces.html

5. 160th Nightstalkers. Retrieved from Army Special Operations: https://goarmysof.com/160th_quals/

6. The Navy definition. Retrieved from the Navy: Navy.com

7. Navy SEALS. Retrieved from Seals/SWCCC: https://www.sealswcc.com/navy-seal-training.html

8. Navy SWCC. Retrieved from Seals/SWCCC: https://www.sealswcc.com/become-navy-swcc.html

9. Navy EOD. Retrieved from the Navy: https://www.navy.com/careers/explosive-ordnance-disposal-technician

10. The Marine definition. Retrieved from the Marines: Marines.com

11. MARSOC Raiders. Retrieved from Military: https://www.military.com/special-operations/marine-corps-marsoc-training.html

12. The Air Force definition. Retrieved from the Air Force: AirForce.com

13. CCT. Retrieved from the United States Air Force Special Tactics: http://www.usafspecialtactics.com/combat-control/

14. PJs. Retrieved from the United States Air Force Special Tactics: http://www.usafspecialtactics.com/pararescue/

15. JSOC. Retrieved from Wikipedia: https://en.wikipedia.org/wiki/Joint_Special_Operations_Command